In The Black 2050

a model for Black economic leadership in the 21st century

By Tre Baker

FIRST EDITION
© 2018 Torch Ventures LLC | All Rights Reserved
intheblack2050.com

In The Black 2050

TABLE OF CONTENTS

DEDICATION	4
PREFACE	5
INTRODUCTION	8
CHAPTER 1	12
Economic State of Black America	
CHAPTER 2	14
Economic Opportunities and Trends in Africa	
CHAPTER 3	17
Organizing Financial and Human Resources	
CHAPTER 4	20
Organizing Domestic Political Power	
CHAPTER 5	30
Organizing International Political Power	
CHAPTER 6	33
Domestic Strategy: Pockets of Independence	
CHAPTER 7	37
International Strategy: Partnering with Africa & the Caribbean	
CHAPTER 8	41
Measuring Success	
CHAPTER 9	46
Pan-African Currency	
CHAPTER 10	51
Language	

CHAPTER 11 **53**
    Development-Focused Investment Strategy
        Venture Capital/Private Equity   54
        Public Equities   58
        Fixed Income   59
        Insurance   60
        Commodities   62
        Real Estate   64
        Cryptocurrency   65

CONCLUSION   **68**

ABOUT THE AUTHOR   **69**

SUGGESTED READING   **70**

DEDICATION

To the ancestors...

Martin Delany, Marcus Garvey, Chancellor Williams, Elijah Muhammad, John Henrik Clarke, Amos Wilson

...and to the youths who march onward and upward toward the light.

PREFACE

While I was in business school, we took a class called BGIE (business, government, and the international economy), which basically analyzed the macroeconomic strategies and resulting performance of various governments around the world. This is when I started to realize that the solutions to the economic problems faced by so-called African Americans become much more clear if you view Black America as a separate nation. This became even more clear when I later read *Blueprint for Black Power* by Amos Wilson, which makes the case in great detail. I hope that this becomes a part of the continuation to his masterful work.

This book is a solutions-oriented guide for Black leaders. This is not an academic paper. It is a guide for practitioners. Throughout Black America and the African diaspora in general we have leaders that consistently ignore the economic reality of our community and make no attempts to provide financially sustainable solutions that aren't dependent on the good graces of Europeans (I'm including so-called white Americans in the European classification). Without a comprehensive, collective economic strategy, everything else we attempt in order to improve our situation will ultimately fail.

Let us look at the example of Tulsa, OK, in the early 1900s (aka

Black Wall Street). If you are not familiar with the history, the documentary *Resurrecting Black Wall Street* does a good job of telling the story of Black Wall Street and its downfall. However, the lesson that we must learn from this story is not how evil racist white people are, but rather that we need to do a better job of defending ourselves and creating resilient systems that can recover when attacked.

Much like being a parent, it is not the parent's job to stop children from exploring and engaging with the world in order to prevent them from breaking things or hurting themselves. A parent should try to anticipate the movements of his/her children and create an environment that will be as safe as possible (e.g. babyproofing), and then set up contingencies for when those safety measures fail or breakdown. You don't stop a child from being a child, you just do your best to make sure that child doesn't hurt herself or others. Compared to older and wiser civilizations, Europeans are like children. It's our job to keep them in check.

For example, the residents who survived the Tulsa massacre wanted to rebuild but their insurance policies (from white insurance companies) wouldn't cover it. Rookie mistake. We should have had our own insurance companies. We don't even need the benefit of hindsight to know that. Europeans have shown us time and again who they are. We know what to expect from them. If we attempt to build a strong Black nation, they WILL absolutely attack it from every angle constantly. The only

In The Black 2050

purpose of a strong Black economy is to provide the resources to build and protect a Black nation, not merely just to accumulate wealth and material possessions to make ourselves more comfortable in our oppression with fancy cars, clothes, and houses.

Marcus Garvey said, "Look for me in the whirlwind or the storm, look for me all around you, for, with God's grace, I shall come and bring with me countless millions of black slaves who have died in America and the West Indies and the millions in Africa to aid you in the fight for Liberty, Freedom and Life."

This is Garvey's whirlwind.

INTRODUCTION

A cursory review of modern history will show that very rarely will a group/community/country achieve sustainable political and social power without economic power. While economic power alone will not solve the Black community's problems, any plan or strategy that does not have a strong economic component will most certainly be a nonstarter. Token political appointments without economic clout behind them are symbolic at best; not very useful for affecting the social or political landscape of a market-driven society. As stated by Dr. Claud Anderson, "Groups with their own economies make wealth-producing decisions in their own best interests. The world is a competitive place and there are few, if any, incentives for other groups to intentionally make decisions in the best interests of Black Americans." And Chancellor Williams states:

> *The economic basis of African life was originally cooperative. Mutual aid was, perhaps, the most significant aspect of the culture. Cooperative undertakings did not stem from any ideology other than commonsense, for them cooperation was one of nature's more important schemes for survival.*

It seems that this common sense is no longer common.

Furthermore, the severe lack or mismanagement of resources can cripple institutional capacity, and both directly and indirectly cause a ripple effect of problems in many other areas of a society (health, education, religion/spirituality, politics/law, etc.). Assuming this basic understanding is correct, Africans and their descendants around the globe must adopt a strategy of cooperative economic self-determination as a prerequisite for the sustainable improvement and continual, positive progression of their existence. Oppressed and under-developed societies throughout history have used various forms of cooperative self-help to improve their standing among other nations.

At its core, an economy is simply a set of relationships between people. For the purposes of this work we are defining economic development as the development of economic systems, which work in concert with social, cultural, and political systems, to fund the advancement of a culture and/or society. The scholarship around Black economic development already exists in significant volume. However, it seems that the Black institutions, and the leaders within them, with the most potential to make use of these insights lack the knowledge, vision and/or strategic direction to capitalise upon them. They rely on 20th century strategies and tactics that are left over from the Civil Rights and Black Power Movements. Hopefully this work can help at least one large organization take a step in the right direction.

It must also be understood that there is significant cultural development work, therapy, and re-education to be done within

In The Black 2050

Africa and the African Diaspora that this paper will not touch on in any depth, but should be addressed by any organization that wishes to follow all or part of this plan, or else the membership will likely have neither the knowledge nor will to see it through. The monumental works by the likes of Chancellor Williams, Amos Wilson, Frances Cress-Welsing, Na'im Akbar, Claud Anderson, Cheikh Anta Diop, Mwalimu Baruti, and John Henrik Clarke, to name a few, would go far in addressing these concerns. This re-education must take place before any sustainable improvements can be maintained.

This point cannot be overstated. The minds of Black people are under constant attack and have been severely damaged. None of the suggestions in this book will make a bit of difference if we do not repair and reclaim our natural African minds.

This is not just about creating jobs and economic opportunities. It's about having the resources to be self-determining and creating our reality as we see fit based on African-centered principles. It is not enough to just replicate European economic systems and compete with them directly. We do not need to look at investments through a purely profit-driven motive. This is not a game of monopoly. We must constantly question the type of systems and culture we want to build.

It is imperative that we operate with a completely different world view in order to create sustainable African-centered societies, and not just put a Black face on white supremacy. We cannot replicate a system that at its core is based on destructiveness, fear, and exploitation and hope to be any better than the primitive beings from which we are attempting to free ourselves.

If you need more convincing on this subject, stop reading this and start with *Know Thyself* by Na'im Akbar and *Afrikan-centered Consciousness vs. The New World Order* by Amos Wilson. Until you have a grasp on the basic differences between African-centered vs. European-centered values and belief systems, it is highly unlikely that you could effectively use the knowledge below to do anything other than perpetuate the oppressive system in which we find ourselves.

As Malcolm X once stated, "The greatest mistake of the movement has been trying to organize a sleeping people around specific goals. You have to wake the people up first, then you'll get action."

CHAPTER 1

Economic State of Black America

We have all heard about the racial disparities in unemployment rates, household income, and household net worth. Further research puts the *real* Black unemployment rate closer to double the official rates, and some communities have experienced over 50% Black unemployment, not to mention underemployment. This is an economic crisis of epidemic proportions.

While the number of Black-owned businesses grew 60% from 2002 to 2007 (approximately 1.9 million businesses in total), more than 1.8 million of those businesses were sole proprietorships with no employees. Combined these businesses produce less than 1% of the nation's GDP. In short, Black business in the United States is insignificant and would hardly be missed if it completely disappeared. This is the singular, fundamental reason for our relative powerlessness to control our economic destinies and the reason we suffer chronic unemployment. Our trillion-dollar buying power is meaningless without our own businesses and institutions on the receiving end of that money. Many other issues and social ills stem from this basic economic problem.

Largely due to integration, the past 50+ years have been focused on getting white people to give us jobs and "jobs training." Why train for jobs that don't exist? During segregation we had our own institutions and businesses and needed very little from the mainstream society. Now we are almost completely dependent. Although reparations for slavery, Jim Crow, land/property theft, and the prison industrial complex are clearly deserved, white people do not have any responsibility to give it to us out of the kindness of their hearts. Power responds to power, not begging. We have to reverse the integrationist mindset and start getting our own economic house in order.

Therefore, we must view Black America as a nation within a nation and build the institutional capacity to manage the economy as such. In the words of Thomas Sowell, "Among the major decisions affecting economic outcomes are decisions about what kinds of enduring institutions a society has for making those decisions - what kind of economic system, operating in what kind of legal system, and controlled by what kind of political system." It could be easily argued that many large, multinational corporations exercise more global influence than many sovereign nation-states. Currently, Black people in America operate in a system in which they exercise very little real control.

CHAPTER 2

Economic Opportunities and Trends in Africa

Finding good investment and employment opportunities for Blacks in America will become increasingly more competitive and difficult. However, the economic opportunities in Africa and the Caribbean are vast, numerous, and constantly evolving, but here are a few relatively recent highlights (source: *African Business Magazine*, multiple 2012 volumes):

- Institutional investors plan to increase their asset allocation in African markets over the next five years. Frontier markets investors are just starting to explore African markets. By 2016, all (out of 158 senior executives surveyed according to the report *Into Africa* by Invest AD and the Economist Intelligence Unit) expect to have some exposure to Africa, with nearly one third expecting to shift at least 5% of their fund value there.
- There is a significant construction boom being fueled by increased political stability, urbanization, resource wealth, and population growth, with the population of the continent said to grow from just over 1bn currently to 2bn by 2050.
- Africa's emerging middle class is catching investors' eyes, ahead of commodities and natural resources.
- Starting a business in Senegal takes 5 days, the same as Canada. Construction permits in Burkina Faso take

98 days, three months faster than the EU.
- The amount of money transacted by M-Pesa in Kenya, which facilitates money transfer through mobile phones, in December 2011 exceed the amount of money Western Union transacted globally.
- Experts estimate Africa would need around $32bn-$39bn annually to achieve full economic potential in its farm sector.
- China is expected to invest more than $100bn in Africa in 2012, more than double the $46bn invested by India. Trade between China and Africa reached over $120bn in 2011, a more than sixfold jump from less than $20bn a decade earlier.
- Around 10% of Africa's landmass is covered by mobile internet services.
- Brazil's overall trade with Africa has quadrupled since 2002 to $20.6bn last year, compared to its $82bn trade with the European Union.
- Africa's total stock market capitalization grew from $245bn in 2002 to more than $1tn in 2010 (~22% CAGR).
- Current ICT spending in sub-Saharan Africa is approx. $70bn and it will nearly double by 2015.
- There are many initiatives underway to increase trade within Africa, including the proposed African Grand Free Trade Area from "Cape to Cairo." Africa currently has 14 regional trading blocs.
- The US plans to invest $1.5bn in the Nigerian power

sector through US private sector firms wishing to work in Nigeria.
- Sub-Saharan Africa attracted $3bn of private equity deals in 2011.
- The African diaspora has around $50bn of savings in Western bank accounts gaining negative returns, adjusted for inflation.
- Ethiopia has implemented several policies to encourage exports, resulting in an increase of 25% each year since 2002 according to the government.
- In Liberia, ArcelorMittal, the world's biggest steel maker, has invested $800m to refurbish an iron ore mine, port, and railways to produce the nation's first exports in the industry.
- South Africa is establishing a venture capital incentive for junior mining companies to strengthen growth in the South African mining sector.

Needless to say, we could fill a large volume with the economic opportunities available in the Caribbean and Africa for enterprising Black people.

CHAPTER 3

Organizing Financial and Human Resources

A Black organization of any significant size (at least 1,000 members) already has the organizational infrastructure in place to mobilize the necessary human and financial capital needed to implement this plan. The first step is for the organization to establish an endowment, which would be entrusted to professional investment managers to invest in a diverse portfolio of financial assets (primarily equities, fixed income, real estate, cryptocurrencies, commodities and venture capital/private equity (VC/PE)), and the returns would be used to fund the organization's operations, member services, and philanthropic/development initiatives. A portion of member dues would be allocated to the endowment along with any outside donations that aren't reserved for a specific project/initiative. This endowment will allow the organization to have a sustainable source of funds and not have to live "hand-to-mouth" with chronic budget deficits or accept money from corporations with strings attached that hinder true Black empowerment. Universities and foundations have long used this strategy.

The next step is for the members to establish investment clubs for small groups or chapters and an overall private investment fund for all members in the organization that choose to participate in the program. These would be for-profit entities that are legally separate from the non-profit organization/endowment. The funds could be invested alongside the endowment, but the returns would benefit the individual members rather than the organization. Then it would be up to the members' discretion as to how much of that profit they donated back to the organization.

Too often Black organizations take resources from their members without providing much value in return while members may be going through hard financial times themselves. Strong members create strong organizations and consistent donors. After these Investment Funds are mobilized, the key will be investing them strategically to achieve the ultimate goal of Black economic independence. Investment managers who receive these funds must be given this mandate and controls must be put in place to make sure they adhere to it. Also, it should go without saying that all uninvested funds should be deposited in Black-owned financial institutions.

Human resources will also be an integral part of the implementation of this plan. Many of these large Black organizations have members with a wide range of managerial and technical expertise that is currently being wasted on "corporate plantations" or in bureaucratic government/academic organizations that stifle their potential and quietly discriminate against them. It is time to unlock this vast human potential for the benefit of the Black community. The first initiative along these lines will be the establishment of an official apprenticeship and rights of passage program where elder members are automatically paired with younger members that have similar personal and professional interests. One of the most valuable assets of any community is the wisdom and experience of its elders. There needs to be a formal system and programs within the organization to facilitate the transmission of this knowledge to various age groups.

These programs should be organized in groups of three age ranges. Each group should consist of one elder, one or two middle-aged members, and two to six younger members. Middle-aged and elder members may have several mentees at a time depending on the demographics of the organization. Rights of passage processes and ceremonies should be implemented to build bonds among peer groups and facilitate deep learning. This will help bridge the generational gap that has developed in the absence of traditional family structures where elders played a larger role, which is a critical component of a healthy, functioning community.

The organization's website should have a members only area where members can access an apprenticeship section which will provide information about the program and the people they are paired with in addition to other sections for job postings, the organization's financial and legal information, membership directory, historical documents, setting up recurring donations, etc. The job posting area would give priority to Black-owned businesses seeking employees, professional services, and private investment.

CHAPTER 4

Organizing Domestic Political Power

The reality is that there does not exist a democracy on the planet that is actually governed by the people. In all systems governing large populations, relatively few people exercise the majority of the power. And, according to Chancellor Williams, "because of the vastness and complex nature of modern societies and the generally indifferent attitude of the people themselves, it could hardly be otherwise. The myth that the people rule is so wonderful and flattering to the people that many have actually come to believe that somehow they do. Reality is concealed by the great stir of elections when candidates for office appeal to them for votes, and the general voting by the people gives them the erroneous feeling that they, the people, are running things through the men they elect to office...Even the candidates for office are generally selected by a few men." This is why Black leadership is so important.

Politics is a component of economics. It decides where a society's resources are focused and redistributed. The Black community's political power can be mobilized to get government resources without "minority" handouts and set-asides using the model of cooperative democracy. Below is an excerpt of a manifesto outlining how this can be accomplished.

In The Black 2050

As the great warrior scholar, Omowale Malcolm X, once said, "We did not land on Plymouth Rock. Plymouth Rock landed on us!" The political system in the United States of America was not created for Black people. On "Independence Day" the vast majority of our ancestors in this country were still enslaved, and that slavery has simply transformed and become more sophisticated and insidious over time. We cannot take our freedom for granted or rely solely on laws created by and for white people to protect and serve us. At no time in this country have we been considered equals or treated with any kind of humanity. Despite popular belief, we were never "given" any rights or freedom. Every inch of progress we have made has come with blood, sweat, and tears. We must exercise our collective political and economic power to stop the genocide being perpetrated against us. As individuals, we are relatively powerless. We are meant to be a communal people as our ancestors were. It's a common saying that the Black community is not a monolith, however, we have been voting as one for decades. It's time we start voting with purpose.

For decades, the Black community has been unwavering in its loyalty to the Democratic party. In exchange for this loyalty we have received benign neglect at best and oftentimes outright betrayal (i.e. the expansion of mass incarceration under the Clinton administration in the 90's). Year after year we give Democrats our *overwhelming support and rarely ask for any meaningful reciprocation. This is due to betrayal by our so-called Black leaders and a lack of organization at all levels. The major Black religious and secular organizations that should be taking the lead on these issues are mired in a slurry of political immaturity, incompetence, corruption, weak leadership, financial mismanagement and outdated thinking left over from the Civil Rights Era. Times have changed. Strategy and tactics must change.*

#BlackLivesMatter has started the process of creating awareness and moving the masses, but lacks strategic direction and has been used as a scapegoat for outside forces that wish to incite violence via the rallies to justify more violence against our people in response. As in the Civil Rights Movement with images of dogs and hoses being used on marchers, they and other social media forces have brought to light the epidemic of police brutality against Black people that has been denied for so long. According to the Black Lives Matter website, "#BlackLivesMatter is an online forum intended to build connections between Black people and our allies to fight anti-Black racism, to spark dialogue among Black people, and to facilitate the types of connections necessary to encourage social action and engagement."

However, awareness, engagement, and protests are only a few tactics that should be employed towards our goals. They are not enough, and they are not how real power is gained. Even pushing for legislative change is not enough. Laws are only as powerful as the ability to enforce them. If the law makers and the people enforcing the laws are intent on breaking them, who will stop them? TheBLOC will focus on organizing and concentrating our political power for the purpose of Black Empowerment and the respect of all life.

TheBLOC is a semi-decentralized collective of Black individuals and organizations that will agree to support political candidates, initiatives that require a vote, and legislation selected/endorsed by theBLOC members based on research and strategy reports from theBLOC members, basically creating a Black voting block. There is no leadership structure and the only central authorities will be moderators in each district that will help verify/approve members and add/monitor proposals put up for a vote to ensure duplicate issues aren't posted and fight spam. How the monitors will be selected/elected will be determined by the membership. In order to become a member, an individual must be a registered voter, invited by another member, and then verified by at least three moderators. While non-Black people cannot be members, those that truly support our cause can vote the same way as theBLOC, as the outcome of all votes will be made available to the public.

TheBLOC is not a political party; it has no party affiliation. It has no political agenda other than organizing and executing the political will of Black people in America and getting something in exchange for our votes. TheBLOC members will vote for whatever party or whatever politician that meets our needs most effectively. It's time we stop giving our votes away and getting nothing in return except lip service.

The decentralization of theBLOC is key to the sustainability and survival of the movement. As we have seen in the past, leaders can be corrupted or killed off and centralized organizations can be infiltrated and divided from within by just a few provocateurs. If there are no leaders, there is no head to cut of the proverbial snake. All digital tools used by theBLOC should be censorship-proof and decentralized in order to prevent single point of failure in its operations.

The primary focus will be districts, cities, and states with large Black populations. Again, the purpose is to concentrate and consolidate our voting power. Members will be organized by voting district and will only be able to vote on items that are relevant to their district. So someone that lives in a district in Atlanta will be able to vote on items related to that district, the city of Atlanta, Fulton County, the state of Georgia, and national/federal items. Votes will take place on a blockchain and each member will receive a private key to ensure one vote per member and prevent results from being manipulated. No physical meetings or rallies should be organized or endorsed by theBLOC. Its sole purpose is to organize Black voting power. We make demands in exchange for our votes and then go to the polls to exercise that power.

Members can suggest issues to put up for a vote along with relevant data, studies, and information in a discussion forum, and if the issue gets enough support (at least 5% of active members in the relevant district, city, state, etc.), a moderator will post it for an official vote. All posted issues should be directly related to a real voting opportunity like an election, bill, etc. and show how the outcome of the vote relates to the Black community. Once results are finalized, a representative from the district, city, state, etc. affected by the vote will be appointed to deliver the results and demands to the relevant elected representatives if necessary. It will be made clear that our votes come with conditions. This person will have no authority to negotiate or make any concessions. They can only receive a response and communicate it to the membership. The response must be recorded (video and audio) or communicated directly from the elected representative in writing or audiovisual recording to prevent any loss in translation from theBLOC representative. Nothing is off the record. No backroom deals can be struck without the membership's knowledge. The membership can then hold another vote based on the new information or stick to the original results and vote accordingly in the actual election/voting opportunity.

For example, in the upcoming Presidential election in America, a forum post could summarize the stances and policies of ALL of the candidates (not just from the two major parties) and their track record with issues that impact the Black community. Similar to a wiki, several members can contribute to the post. Ideally, along with all the in-depth research, there will be a standard set of criteria that candidates will be judged on, summarized in a side-by-side comparison. Once that post has been upvoted enough times, then a vote will be put up for the election with a link to the forum post for members' reference as we want to encourage informed voting.

However, before the actual vote takes place, all candidates that receive over 10% of the votes will be contacted by the appointed moderator and given a chance to address our members' concerns. We will share with them the criteria we are using for the side-by-side comparison and they can tell us how they will address each issue/demand raised by our membership. For example, Black unemployment, mass incarceration, government contracts for Black-owned businesses, environmental justice in Black communities, and reparations could all be possible issues that would be presented for response. A final vote will be posted once all responses have been received. Regardless of a member's individual vote, they will then agree to vote for whoever wins theBLOC vote.

Our ancestors died to secure our voting rights, but voting with no strategy, organization, and specific goals is a waste of that sacrifice. It is high time we start getting real value that benefits our community in exchange for our votes.

As this system does not use political parties as a pretense for choice, there is no need for an opposition party because opposition is built into the fabric of the system where ideas compete on equal footing and leaders are judged by their ability to formulate and execute their plans with validation and direction from the people.

It is worth noting that a similar strategy could be implemented on a small scale to govern the Black organizations this plan is targeting. Technology can be leveraged to create efficient administrative, polling/voting, and governance systems that keep members engaged and empowered while also holding leadership accountable. Needless to say, the Black community and many large Black organizations, institutions, and governments suffer from a lack of effective leadership and many have outdated missions/goals. Financial mismanagement, incompetence, and often outright fraud are rampant among these organizations. People must hold their leaders to a higher standard.

Before any of the suggestions in this book can be implemented within an organization, a serious evaluation of the leadership must be conducted and members need to clean house. Leaders with eurocentric values and ideals must go. There's no way around this. One hallmark of eurocentrism is extreme individualism. Individuals are easily corrupted, and there is no place for this among leaders in a democracy. Individualism is a fantasy perpetuated by ego. Interconnectedness is the reality, which should be recognized by any leader worthy of our support.

Leaders who are comfortable and complacent in their positions of relative power, who simply wish to maintain the status quo must go because nowhere on the planet is the status quo good enough for our people. Williams states, "That the wrong man is often mistaken for a true leader and political power thus misplaced is a fact of common experience. Democracy's safeguard in all such cases should be the African safeguard through quick destoolment. Where this safeguard prevails, the arbitrary abuse of power cannot prevail."

The proof is in the pudding as they say, so if there has been no significant progress made towards the mission of the organization, then the first place that needs to be reformed is the leadership and administration. Missions must also be re-evaluated, updated, and tested against the needs of the community it serves. How does the vision for the organization compliment the vision of self-determination and empowerment for the Black community? If it doesn't directly relate to one of those two things, then we don't need that organization and those resources would be better spent elsewhere.

CHAPTER 5

Organizing International Political Power

What is also needed is an international organization (or several) that can act on behalf of so-called African Americans. It could be called the African American International Cooperation Agency (AAICA), modeled after the Japan International Cooperation Agency.

JICA has offices all over the world and assists in various humanitarian and development works with a focus on long-term outcomes. They send people to various countries so they can have boots on the ground and learn exactly what is needed at a local level. Their mission is to "work on human security and quality growth," and their vision is to "take the lead in forging bonds of trust across the world, aspiring for a free, peaceful and prosperous world where people can hope for a better future and explore their diverse potentials."

As previously mentioned, Black Americans have a wide range of skills and talents that have heretofore been used primarily for the benefit of non-Black companies and organizations. Employing even a fraction of this human capital to help development efforts in Black communities around the world would have a significant impact and garner political good will needed for substantive international negotiations on behalf of African Americans and the

Diaspora.

Since food water and shelter are problems in many countries around the world, an obvious first project could be to develop sustainable communities that address energy production water harvesting/purification and sustainable housing in a decentralized and resilient fashion. Something similar to the Sahara Forest Project that combines food, energy, and water production, but adding mixed-use real estate and incorporating it all into urban and suburban environments in addition to rural villages. The technology already exists to take on this project and there are examples we can look to and improve upon. Just imagine how our standing around the world would improve if we went around providing food, energy, shelter, and water while training the local populations how to do the same for themselves along with military training to defend what they've built.

This and much more could be accomplished by the AAICA, which would position it to claim a seat at the table in the African Union, which, as a part of the Sixth Region initiative, allows for the accreditation and participation of Diaspora organizations and networks as observers, delegates and participants at AU Summit and other meetings. The Sixth Region represents the African Diaspora, which the African Union defines as "Consisting of people of African origin living outside the continent, irrespective of their citizenship and nationality and who are willing to contribute to the development of the continent and the building of the African Union." Its constitutive act declares that it shall "invite and encourage the full participation of the African Diaspora as an important part of our continent, in the building of the African Union."

According to Michelle DeFreese, "At the 2012 Global African Diaspora Summit, organizers released a declaration reiterating the relevance of the Sixth Region. The document placed an emphasis on the Diaspora, calling on its representatives to 'organize themselves in regional networks and establish appropriate mechanisms that will enable their increasing participation in the affairs of the African Union as observers and eventually, in the future, as a Sixth Region of the continent that would contribute substantially to the implementation of policies and programs.'" In short, our participation has been requested, and we need to create organizations that are capable of representing our interests, or else the Sixth Region will continue to play a mostly symbolic role in the AU and not have any substantive effect regarding policy and leadership.

For such an organization, whether AAICA or another entity, to play a meaningful role in the African Union it will have to have a clear leadership structure with well-defined roles and objectives as well as efficient and effective governance procedures that are transparent, democratic, and corruption resistant. With the advent of blockchain-based decentralized organization management systems, this process is now possible at scale.

CHAPTER 6

Domestic Strategy: Pockets of Independence

There are several cities and towns around the country where Blacks represent a majority or near-majority of the population, yet still behave as minorities when it comes to political strategy, begging for minority set-asides. Why would a majority population still ask for minority handouts? Majorities should control the majority of the social, political, and economic resources in their area. The majority of government contracts should be allocated to the majority group. It is time to start strategically concentrating our numbers in key locations around the country where we already have sizable populations. This can be accomplished by re-locating Black-controlled businesses to these areas and creating jobs (in the public and private sectors) to attract even more people to them.

> *Black Americans were brought to this country to be a labor force. Their problem is not the lack of jobs. The lack of jobs is a symptom of their lack of wealth and businesses that produce jobs.*
> -Dr. Claud Anderson

Once these geographic areas are identified, members should begin by acquiring real estate in key locations throughout the city in predominantly Black neighborhoods in order to develop mixed-use communities where people can live, work, and socialize all in the same vicinity (similar to Atlantic Station in Atlanta, GA). Formal "sister city" programs and trade relations should be established between these cities and other cities in Africa and the Caribbean. Ownership of land and securing local building materials, food, and water resources are key. These locations should be cultural hubs with art, museums, parks, and other tourist attractions to encourage Black tourism.

Businesses that are not Black-owned in Black neighborhoods outside of the mixed-use communities described above should also be taken over or shut down and repurposed. Each such business should be strategically boycotted and pressured to sell, driving down the value of the business and encouraging the owner to sell it at a discounted price or forcing them out of business. The businesses will be acquired using financing from the endowments, local investment clubs, Black-owned banks, and Black employees. Each business in the community should be primarily owned by its employees and members of the community to ensure equitable distributions of wealth and prevent the concentration of power in few hands. In addition to being more equitable, employee-owned companies have been shown to be more productive and profitable according to several studies available from the National Center for Employee Ownership.

In addition to residential and commercial developments, a heavy focus should be placed on agriculture and, particularly, sustainable urban farming. If we can't feed ourselves, we will always be at the mercy of those who can. As the grandson of a farmer, this is especially apparent to me. My family was never "rich" but we used to grow/raise the majority of food we ate. That is true freedom. Now the technology exists that will allow people to grow food economically indoors all year around. There is no reason for our food supply to be dependent on weather anymore.

We can take over abandoned buildings and lots to create vertical farms near where we live. This increases the resilience of our food supply and reduces the energy needed to transport it to where it's needed, such as Black-owned grocery stores and restaurants.

As we've seen too often in the past when Black communities have achieved some level of economic success, they become targets of terrorism by whites. Therefore, private security companies should be established to train and employ people in the community (primarily young Black men and women) and provide security services to local Black businesses and neighborhoods in the network. Local youth and military veterans should be trained and employed by this security company with the benefit of providing the youth with employment and discipline. All personal and business property should be secured from external and internal threats.

All Black-owned businesses in the target areas should be required to contribute a small portion of revenue to the endowment and local non-profits benefiting the Black community in a sustainable manner. In exchange, they will receive access to debt and equity financing from the investment clubs and investment funds, marketing support, and social legitimacy to operate within the community.

CHAPTER 7

International Strategy: Partnering with Africa & the Caribbean

A minority community within another country will rarely achieve political autonomy or control (the exceptions to this rule usually result in oppressive behavior by that minority, e.g. South African apartheid). The power of sovereignty in the modern geopolitical landscape cannot be underestimated. A representative acting on behalf of a sovereign government will hold more weight on the international stage and in the global economy than representatives from even the largest Black organizations. While minorities are protected, the majority generally rules. Any advances that we do make will come only after a great deal of effort and friction. However, as African citizens, we would be able to truly be self-determining and respected on the world stage.

While we may not choose to fully abandon the country that we have come to call home, we must acknowledge that without sufficient political and economic control, the destiny of the African American community will be subject to the whims of the majority. Whether we choose to help save America from its current decline or focus on just saving ourselves, it cannot be denied that our political position would be enhanced by partnering with the increasingly important governments in what are now called frontier markets, but will soon become developed markets due to their vast resource wealth and increasing political influence. African Americans and other African descendents in the Diaspora are in the best place to take advantage of their natural connection to Africa and form a mutually beneficial, synergistic relationship.

Furthermore, from a purely self-interested, financial point of view, there are vast economic opportunities in Africa that are already being exploited by Western powers in addition to the resource hungry BRIC nations. There is no reason why Africa's long lost sons and daughters should not be involved in these opportunities, as we have a common ancestry and genuine interest in the sustainable social and economic development of these countries, rather than the pure resource extraction focus of other groups/countries/companies currently clamoring for Africa's riches.

Therefore, a formal economic alliance between major Black organizations in the Diaspora and the African Union should be established as a part of the Sixth Region initiative. The Sixth Region (the African Diaspora) should be an officially recognized political entity funded by its member organizations with member benefits, including, but not limited to: an expedited path to dual citizenship in participating countries, free/subsidized land, membership in the African Union, and economic incentives for repatriating and/or investing in participating countries. In return, the participating countries will receive an influx of human and intellectual capital, increased revenue/tax base, and source of both long-term and short-term investment funds.

Since Africa is currently importing the skills, technical and organizational capabilities necessary for the massive infrastructure and industrial expansion underway, the knowledge and skills we would bring to the table alone would be sufficient incentive for the partner countries in Africa to agree to this scheme. There has been a massive brain drain on the continent that is slowly being reversed. We could turn that trickle into a flood of intellectual capacity. Furthermore, we could use our political influence in countries with large Diaspora populations to encourage favorable trade policies for the participating countries, opening up developed markets for goods and services from those countries.

If not currently in existence, sovereign wealth funds will be established in the participating countries and invested alongside the investment funds established by the Black organizations in the Diaspora. Investment returns from the funds should be used to supplement government spending and reduce the tax burden on citizens. And since sovereign wealth funds tend to have a longer-term investment horizon and lower hurdle rates with emphasis on both financial and nonfinancial returns, the returns of the for-profit investment funds can be leveraged up. The organization of all the proposed funds are diagrammed below using Liberia as an example.

Diagram

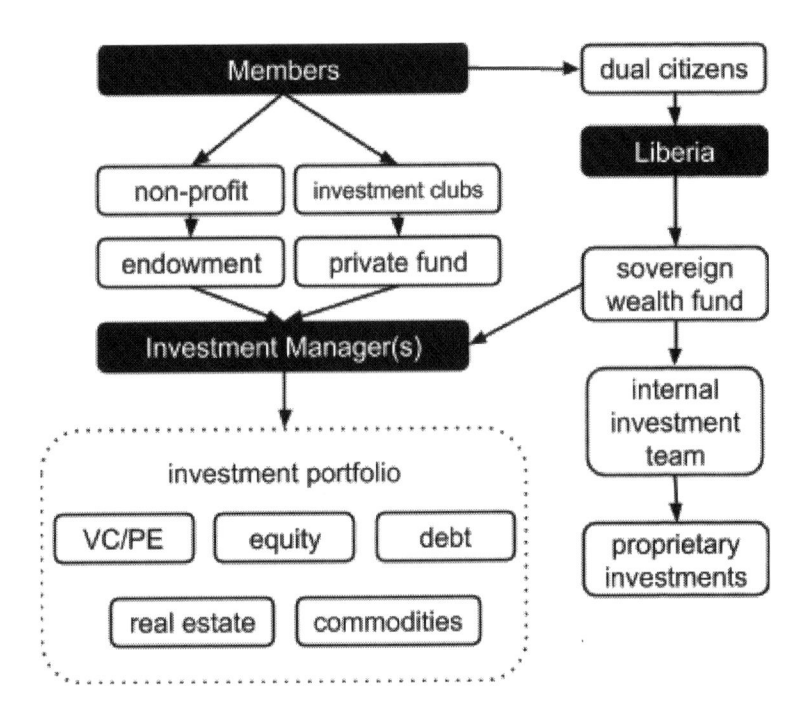

```
Members → dual citizens
          Liberia
Members → non-profit → endowment → Investment Manager(s)
Members → investment clubs → private fund → Investment Manager(s)
Liberia → sovereign wealth fund → Investment Manager(s)
sovereign wealth fund → internal investment team → proprietary investments

Investment Manager(s) → investment portfolio:
  VC/PE, equity, debt, real estate, commodities
```

To recap, the members contribute to for-profit and non-profit investment funds, which are all managed by professional investment managers in various asset classes, who will also assist countries in managing a portion of their their sovereign wealth funds, which will also be contributed to indirectly by members who have obtained citizenship in the participating countries. However, the sovereign wealth funds will be independent entities as well, so they may not always invest along with the member-contributed funds.

CHAPTER 8

Measuring Success

In order to effectively implement these strategies we must define our own measures of success. Concepts like GDP, profit margins, and net present value are primitive and inadequate measures of the success or failure of individual, company, and national economic decisions. We cannot use Eurocentric definitions and concepts to define our success. A new system requires a new set of terms.

Let's start with the big one. According to Investopedia, "The gross domestic product (GDP) is one of the primary indicators used to gauge the health of a country's economy. It represents the total dollar value of all goods and services produced over a specific time period; you can think of it as the size of the economy." This last phrase, "the size of the economy," is problematic when you look at what is included in this so-called definition of an economy.

The formula for GDP is: GDP = C + I + G + (Ex - Im), where "C" equals spending by consumers, "I" equals the sum of all the country's investments, "G" is government spending and "(Ex - Im)" equals net exports, in other words, the value of exports minus imports. Net exports may be negative, as they have likely been in the Black community for decades.

That last term, net exports, is actually very important to the global African community as our first priority should be import substitution. When you import anything, money leaves your community. When consumers in the United States buy Chinese goods, they use money to pay for it. Thus, China gets U.S. dollars, and the U.S. gets products. Over time, if we continue to import more than we export, more and more money will leave the U.S., but this money has to come from somewhere. If it doesn't come from exports to other countries, then it will have to come from debt, which will involve printing more money and increasing inflation. Long-term, this is unsustainable for an economy and why you see the U.S. with such a large deficit now. In order to reverse this process, you must reduce imports and/or increase exports.

The problem with focusing on increasing exports rather than reducing imports comes when you are heavily importing products/services in key industries necessary for survival, like food, water, construction materials, and energy. If you rely too much on imports in these industries, you run the risk of losing the ability for your domestic economy to take care of the basic needs of its people and you become completely reliant on outside forces for your survival. This is the situation African people around the world find themselves in, and, needless to say, it is a terrible strategic position. African people should therefore initially focus on producing more of the things that they already buy in significant numbers, also known as import substitution.

However, if we just look at net exports without putting it through an African-centered filter, we may just create an equally unsustainable system, but controlled by Africans instead of Europeans or Asians. For example, if our only concern is increasing exports we may be tempted to start with industries in which Black people are large consumers rather than the core sectors discussed below. Thus, instead of securing our food supply, land/shelter, and other basic necessities we might start producing luxury clothing, liquor, or owning fast food franchises without farming and processing the food sold in them. While these are all potentially lucrative businesses, they do not allow us to be economically independent or self-sufficient and should not be priorities.

Concerning consumer spending in the GDP formula, while useful information in general, it is misleading to use as a component of the health of an economy. First, there is no emphasis anywhere in the formula on uninvested savings and having a large consumption number without knowing how much is being saved does not give an accurate picture of the long-term financial health of consumers. Second, "bad" things can increase consumption, for example, healthcare spending. GDP in general overemphasizes growth for growth's sake, whether or not it's good or bad. Grow the economy by any means.

For example, most people would agree that a natural disaster that causes mass injuries and property damage would be a bad thing, but that would increase hospital revenue from treating the victims injuries, increased casket sales for the inevitable funerals that follow the disaster, and increased spending on construction materials and labor to rebuild and repair the damage. These things would all increase the consumer spending component of the GDP formula but are not necessarily indicators of "good" economic performance because those financial and human resources could have gone towards investing and building for the future. Finally, using debt to fund consumer spending is generally not good for a sustainable economy, however that is not taken into consideration in the GDP formula.

Granted, GDP is not meant to be the end-all-be-all of economic indicators, but it is the main one quoted in the press and in the minds of the average person. What gets measured gets improved. Increasing GDP by increasing wasteful government spending or debt-financed consumer spending would both work, but those things should not indicate "good" economic performance if you are concerned with sustainability, efficiency and/or the long-term economic health of the nation and individual households. GDP also does not account for natural resources. For example, trees and plants perform some very valuable functions including converting CO_2 into oxygen, filtering water, fixing soil, and preventing erosion. Fresh water is perhaps one of the world's most precious resources and it is only accounted for in GDP by how much we pay for, not how much is actually used or how much is left. Using GDP to measure an economy is like gauging someone's health based on how much they eat, assuming the more they eat, the better, which we all know is not the case.

We must therefore take an African-centered approach. This should be a major endeavor of African-centered scholars and economists worthy of a think tank solely dedicated to the task. Some of the basic tenets of African-centeredness would be prioritizing the collective over the individual while still valuing every individual life, maintaining balance and reciprocity in all things, environmental sustainability as a way of life rather than an afterthought, recognizing the interconnectedness of all things and past/present/future. Viewed in this light, an overall measure of an economy should include the level of long-term savings, the value of the nation's natural resources (minerals, precious metals, fossil fuels, trees, fresh water, sunlight, etc.), business investments, individual investments, investments in education, something to measure the health and happiness of the population, etc. That said, this number will most likely not be just a dollar value, although it may be possible to place an approximate dollar value on most of the components.

Some current alternatives to GDP have already been proposed, such as Green GDP, Gross National Happiness, Green Growth, Plenitude Economics, etc. We must also come up with our own indicators to measure political, social, and cultural factors. It's not enough to just succeed economically if we are creating society no better than Europeans, who value profit over humanity, nature, and culture.

CHAPTER 9

Pan-African Currency

The intention is not to go too deep into basic economics, but there is a general, widespread ignorance about how money fundamentally works and what gives money "value," and this must be understood before we can have a productive discussion on how to design a currency or monetary system.

First, money has no fundamental value. For example, the United States Dollar is backed by nothing but the "full faith and credit" of the U.S. government. In other words, it's backed by nothing. It is essentially an IOU that only has value because we agree it does, but that value is relative and constantly shifting because of monetary policy and economic trends. Even when the world's major currencies were backed by gold, what was gold backed by? Nothing. Gold has very little utility for anyone outside the electronics industry. Even gold jewelry has no real value. In a real crisis, a water filter has much more utility than a brick of gold. You can't eat or drink gold, but we all agree that it is "valuable."

However, now that all the world's major currencies aren't backed by gold or any physical assets, we call them fiat currencies. Monetary systems that use fiat currencies are usually run by central banks. For example, the central bank in United States is called the Federal Reserve (aka the Fed). These institutions are usually independent from the federal government and are responsible for managing a country's money supply and interest rates. Now this is where the insidious nature of this modern economic system comes into play.

Central banks have instituted what is called fractional reserve banking. The US government doesn't actually issue money, except physical coins. When it needs to raise money, it basically takes out a loan in exchange for money with the promise to repay at a later date. So already a house of cards is being built because from day 1 there is not enough money in the economy to pay off the debt, so more money needs to be created. That's where fractional banking comes into play.

In order to increase money supply directly, the central bank purchases debt instruments from commercial banks. Where does it get the money to buy the debt? If it doesn't already have the money, then it creates the money from thin air. This is what begins the process of increasing the money supply. It buys the debt and credits the banks that sold it. Now that bank has new money on its balance sheet. Because of the fractional reserve system, that bank is now allowed to loan out more than they actually received. In the United States this ratio is 10%, so for every $100 they receive, they can loan out $90. Then the person who receives that $90 deposits it in a bank, and that bank can loan out $81 and so on. Now by adding $100 to a bank, you've added much more than $100 to the money supply.

Now the Fed can reverse this process to remove money from the supply, but over the long-term it rarely does this. They actually have an inflation target, which means they are constantly increasing the money supply on average over time. They have to constantly increase the money supply to service the debt created when the money is created, but for every additional dollar created, the value of all other dollars goes down if demand for dollars does not also rise. This is why inflation is a hidden tax on all people using dollars. The Fed is literally taking value away from all of our dollars when it creates additional dollars.

Despite the fundamentally unsustainable and unfair nature of this debt-based system, central banks simply do not have the real-time information needed to make the decisions they are tasked to make to influence the money supply. They are constantly playing a game of catch up. Human error is inevitable.

In order to have a truly independent economy, we must have control of our money supply, keeping in mind that currency should be used to store and transmit value, not as a means for a central authority to manipulate the economy. If the monetary system is set up properly, there will be no need to manipulate the money supply.

When creating our own currency, the following attributes of an ideal currency should be kept in mind:

- Durable - can be used many times without degrading
- Portable - easy to move around and transfer
- Divisible - can broken down into smaller units
- Hard to counterfeit
- Generally accepted by the population
- Stability of value over time

A Pan-African monetary system should be developed in order to help create economic unity within Africa and separate ourselves from the unsustainable debt-based monetary systems that currently serve as the global status quo.

The currencies of individual African countries are not strong enough to compete on a global scale, and will inevitably shift with the winds blown by other, stronger currencies. While individual countries may maintain their own sovereign currencies for the time being, an effort should be made to establish a unified currency or small group of currencies that are easily exchanged amongst each other and can be used to facilitate trade between participating countries. This would be similar to the Euro, except controlled by Africans and completely digital and decentralized, like Bitcoin, so no one nation or entity can control it. Obviously there will need to be more cooperation among African countries beyond regional trade blocs to make this happen.

Businesses owned by Blacks in the Diaspora should also accept this currency from customers and use it to pay employees and suppliers whenever possible, and investment funds should eventually be denominated in this Pan-African currency. Black-owned exchanges should be set up to convert this currency into other digital and fiat currencies.

One organization, BlacKrypto Society, has started this process of organizing the Black community around various cryptocurrency investment initiatives and created the first Black crypto coin with actual utility, the BLKS coin. At the time of this writing, it can be used to invest in masternodes, ICOs, a crypto ETF and used to purchase products from various Black-owned businesses. There's also CJs, started by the founders of the social media community Wacoinda, which has complementary goals, and GUAP coin, which is meant to be a payment method for Black-owned businesses. These and other cryptocurrencies and crypto assets that are developed in the future should have our full support if we ever expect to gain true economic independence.

CHAPTER 10

Language

Language is an often overlooked aspect of business. It is no wonder that countries that share a common language tend to trade with each other more often. In addition to being a unifier, language is also a powerful transmitter of culture.

Business and government in Africa should be conducted in a common African language. Other local and foreign languages may still be spoken as secondary languages, but all schools should teach one African language as the primary language so that anyone who wishes to conduct business or deal with the government/legal system must speak the language. Obviously this will be a difficult task to unify all of Africa under a common language, but it must be done. This language must be an African language, because, as stated by Cheikh Anta Diop, "Linguistic unity based on a foreign language, however one may look at it, is cultural abortion. It would irremediably eventuate in the death of the authentic national culture, the end of our deeper intellectual and spiritual life and reduce us to perpetual copycats, having missed out on our historical mission in this world."

Therefore, the goal of any organization wishing to participate in this plan should be to promote the learning of this common language, once decided upon, to its members at a minimum and ultimately throughout Africa and the Diaspora. Swahili would be the obvious choice due to the educational resources already developed for it and its status as the most widely spoken African language, but going into a deep dive on African linguistics is beyond the scope of this work.

CHAPTER 11

Development-Focused Investment Strategy

Once an organization or group of organizations has set up the aforementioned infrastructure/partnerships to mobilize financial and human capital, that capital will need to be managed and deployed by professional investment management companies with the primary strategy of building industries and consolidating markets via platform investments and vertical integration with a Pan-African and environmentally responsible focus. Investments should be made in the strategic asset classes and industries we will outline below, and driven by the principles of sustainability (energy and resource efficiency), resilience (ability to withstand external shocks), and biomimicry (applying lessons from existing organisms and life systems/processes which have been tested and adapted over billions of years).

Environmental and social governance must be a key part of any investment or management decision. We can no longer afford to operate under the assumption of inexhaustible resources without considering the total systems (industrial and ecological) and product life cycles, from cradle-to-cradle. Earth is a closed system where nothing is wasted, and our business systems should achieve the same outcome. Furthermore, the latest advances in areas like green technology and biomimicry are showing us that not only are better social and ecological outcomes possible from environmentally responsible business practices, but there are also opportunities to create and capture more financial value as well through the innovation that these advances encourage. Intuitively, it is easy to see how concepts like zero waste can increase financial returns because waste is indicative of operational inefficiencies, therefore, reducing or eliminating it should boost productivity in many cases. In short, investment opportunities should be evaluated from financial, social, and environmental perspectives.

Venture Capital/Private Equity

Black-owned private equity/venture capital firms already exist. The reader may be wondering why we need to start another one. The answer is that, while the existing firms are managed by very capable and experienced executives, none have reached any significant scale or made a material impact on the economic well-being of the Black community. I believe this is due to a lack of differentiation and specific focus on the Black community as an emerging market. They are attempting to compete with undifferentiated strategies directly in a field that is saturated with competition that has the very real advantage of white privilege and intergenerational wealth. Also, a cursory look at their portfolio companies shows a lack of strategic portfolio management regarding the synergies between portfolio companies. For any Black private equity firm to have a significant impact, it cannot merely replicate the strategies of "mainstream" firms; it must have a mission that allows it to exploit its status as a Black-owned firm as a competitive advantage rather than an impediment. We are not suggesting that the existing firms adopt our strategy if their current strategy is working for them (i.e. producing above-average returns). We are merely suggesting that Black investments firms, rather than competing in a crowded "red ocean" of existing players and investment strategies, should consider operating in the "blue ocean" of investing with the goal of Black economic self-determination.

When viewed as a developing market, the parallels between Black America and emerging/frontier markets in Africa become clear. In developing markets around the world, private investments can be used to build infrastructure and core industries (finance, food, energy, water, housing, distribution, transportation, security, etc.), which is the foundation for even greater growth. This is what is needed in predominantly Black communities in America as well; however, most Black-owned businesses (and the few funds that invest in them) are focused on non-essential consumer goods, technology, entertainment, and services. This is a result of the assumption that Blacks have been fully integrated into America, and can therefore afford to focus on superfluous, individual opportunities rather than coordinated strategic investments. That assumption has been proven to be false, and to continue operating under it is to ignore the huge potential investment opportunities within our own communities.

Private equity can be used to enhance the value of portfolio companies through financial engineering, operational efficiency improvements, and accelerating organic growth. Furthermore, in this case, the resulting increased cash flow from organic growth can be used to help fund inorganic growth through acquisition. The Investment Funds should focus on platform investments in mid-market to large-cap companies that can be used to break into an industry and start acquiring smaller competitors and related adjacent businesses (horizontal integration) as well as other firms in the supply chain (vertical integration) once sufficient scale is achieved.

This vertical integration should begin as far downstream as possible (closest to the customer), preferably at the retail level, except in the cases of extremely supply constrained industries. The problem many Black-owned producers/manufacturers run into is getting retail distribution. The obvious solution to this problem is to control access to the customer. Once buying power has been enhanced and consolidated through organic and inorganic growth, the Investment Funds and the platform company can begin to integrate upstream all the way to production of raw materials.

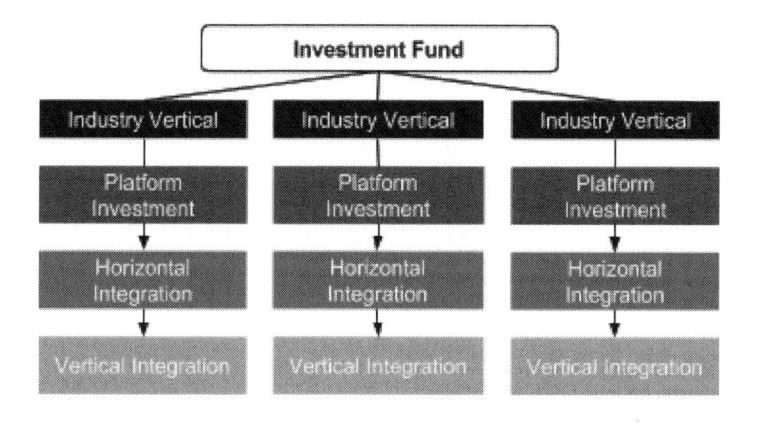

```
                    Investment Fund
         ┌──────────────┼──────────────┐
   Industry Vertical  Industry Vertical  Industry Vertical
         │              │              │
      Platform       Platform       Platform
     Investment     Investment     Investment
         │              │              │
     Horizontal     Horizontal     Horizontal
     Integration    Integration    Integration
         │              │              │
   Vertical Integration  Vertical Integration  Vertical Integration
```

Let's look at the food industry as an example to use with this model. A medium to large grocery chain would be acquired first (platform investment), and then smaller local chains or individual stores could be acquired to expand horizontally and achieve higher economies of scale. Once demand has been sufficiently aggregated, then vertical integration can begin by acquiring food distribution and logistics companies, processing plants, and farms.

Due to the new JOBS Act, it will be easier for startups and small companies to raise money from non-accredited investors. This opens up the opportunity to combine PE funds with investments from individuals in the community. The endowments and private funds mentioned above can be used to make initial investments in Black-owned businesses, or to purchase non-Black-owned businesses so that they become Black-owned. Then once the portfolio companies are ready to take on more capital, a portion of it can be raised from employees and members of the community where they have a physical presence (similar to an IPO). This will cause members of the community to have a vested interest in the success of the company, as well as a voice/vote to prevent the company from engaging in behavior that may be destructive to that community (pollution, employment discrimination, etc.).

Public Equities

Sometimes it makes more sense to take over existing publicly-traded companies rather than attempting to build new ones or buy private enterprises. Equity investments should be made in companies that are potential takeover targets in the industries identified herein using a value investment strategy. Preference will be given to companies with higher dividend yields and a history of consistent dividend payments. Hedge funds may also be used to capitalize on arbitrage opportunities, special situations, and dislocated markets.

The Investment Funds will slowly build positions in target companies, while earning dividends, until sufficient voting power has been achieved and there is a high probability that a leveraged buyout (LBO) can be successfully executed. While the Investment Funds still own a minority share, they can still be used to influence board positions and key executive hires before the takeover attempt. With this and other large investments in currently non-Black-owned assets, the use of caucasian "straw men" to represent the Investment Funds may be necessary in certain scenarios.

There is actually a precedent for something like this that happened in South Africa. Amos Wilson writes in his monumental book, *Blueprint for Black Power*:

> "For example, Afrikan South Afrikan, Donald Ncube, former executive and board member of Anglo-American, South Afrika's largest conglomerate, assembled an unusual group of investors to acquire majority ownership of African Life, a formerly White-owned insurance company which caters essentially to the Black market. Ncube acquired 51% of the company by going to 'black organizations that control money and assets but are outside the traditional financial market. They include trade unions, church groups, trusts and Stokvels or community pools of money that were set up to allow blacks to get around the lack of bank financing.'

Secondarily, investments should also be made in a wide array of short term investment strategies through various Black fund managers with proven track records.

Fixed Income

Debt is used primarily to lower a company's total cost of capital and provide leverage in order to increase equity returns while offering stable returns to the debt providers. The strategy here will simply be to invest in the debt of African and Caribbean countries and companies as well as convertible debt in the companies in which the Investment Funds invest. Debt usually receives a higher priority in the capital structure of a company over equity, therefore, lower risk. Obviously, stringent underwriting standards will need to be used given the higher perceived risk inherent in these areas.

An indirect and extremely profitable way of investing in debt would actually be to acquire a bank, or several. Banks take customer deposits and lend them out for various types of loans. Due to the fractional reserve system, banks must hold 10% of their assets in reserve, so they can loan out $9 for every $1 in deposits they receive. So if a community was able to come together and collectively deposit $1,000,000 into a bank, that bank could then make $9,000,000 in loans. Obviously this is a great way to leverage capital to benefit the community.

Other fixed income strategies include investing in treasuries, municipal and corporate bonds, which should be pursued specifically for treasuries/municipal bonds from countries/cities where the strategy outlined in this book has been implemented and corporate bonds of Black-owned companies.

Insurance

Almost every person in the United States has or had at least some kind of insurance, but very few people understand why it's such a profitable industry. Similar to banks that get to loan money they don't actually have, insurance companies get to invest money that isn't technically theirs.

The insurance company's customers all pay regular premiums, usually monthly. So they are giving the insurance company money every month, but the company only has to pay it out when there is a claim. Most people go long periods of time or never actually file a claim, and they end up paying for insurance they never use (the exception would be life insurance because we all die at some point). Insurance companies have sophisticated formulas to calculate the claims they are likely to have to pay. They usually make a profit on the premiums they collect versus the claims the pay out, unless a large natural disaster or unforeseen catastrophe happens that affects the whole market in which they operate.

However, just as an example, let's say the insurance companies eventually pay out all the money they collect. There's still a time lag between when they collect the money and when they pay it out. During that time they are investing that money, known as the float. So if they collect $100 and invest it, making a 2% return in a year and then have to pay out the $100 for a claim, like a car accident, they still made $2 off that $100 before they had to pay it out. The insurance industry invests *trillions* of dollars this way, effectively earning billions in investment profits on money that isn't technically theirs.

You can see why this is an industry we need to be involved in; not to mention the fact that these insurance companies have a long track record of racist practices against Black people. A great illustration of this can be found in *Black Titan* about A.G. Gaston, one of the wealthiest Black men during the Civil Rights Era, who actually made most of his money in the insurance business and used it to help fund the movement.

The easiest place to start would be with life insurance and car insurance. All the Black-owned insurance companies that operate in each market should be identified, and Black consumers should be incentivized to switch their business to them and help grow these existing companies. For less common insurance products like general liability for small businesses where existing Black-owned providers may not exist, the market potential and current competitive landscape should be explored and potential acquisitions should be identified. If suitable acquisitions do not exist in the markets with the most market potential and relevance to the insurance needs of the Black community, new companies can be established.

Commodities

Africa is prized for its natural resources, which is where most of the financial activity on the continent has originated. Proper management of these resources is key to sustainable economic growth. Unlike consumer industries, the key with commodities is to build ownership interests as close to the source as possible and do as much value-added processing in-house as possible before selling to end-users. Most likely this will require working closely with governments as they are usually very involved in extractive industries. It will be critical to integrate down the supply chain when possible and add value to these commodities before domestic use or international export.

Furthermore, since the commodities come from land that belongs to a country's citizens, the citizens should benefit from their extraction and sale. A portion of the profits from any deal struck to remove a country's natural resources should go to the sovereign wealth funds mentioned previously. This will ensure that even though the resources are sold off, they will continue to provide financial returns in the years to come.

Under this same umbrella, agriculture in Africa is still king. Agriculture currently employs about 65% of Africa's labor force and accounts for 32% of GDP according to the World Bank. However, the technological advancement of the agricultural sector has stagnated and is in need of serious reform. The latest advances in sustainable, organic farming techniques could not only feed all of Africa's population, but produce a sufficient surplus for exports. Vertical/indoor farming, no-till farming, hydroponics, and aquaponics all have the ability to significantly improve crop yields and quality. Land is no longer a constraint when it comes to food production.

In addition to improving the efficiency of farming, we must create more efficient markets for small farmers to sell their goods. Large, centralized distribution is the thing of the past. Local distribution is more suitable for a sustainable future. In order to accomplish this, farmers must have access to real-time information on prices and quality required for local markets and distribution channels. Several apps have been developed to address this and supply chain technology is constantly improving, making an efficient, decentralized food system technically feasible.

Real Estate

The main focus of the real estate investments should be long-term strategies consisting of land aggregation for agriculture and infrastructure, energy/mining exploration, industry, and the development of planned, mixed-use communities in the Southeast US (in areas with at least 20% Black populations), the Caribbean, and Africa to support our other investments. However, traditional investments in rental properties, REITS, and real estate debt should also be pursued as short term strategies. Again, the highest environmental standards should be used when planning and constructing these developments, and brownfield sites should be remediated and revitalized whenever possible. Much of Africa is undeveloped, so we have a chance to start with a clean slate rather than dealing with legacy (unsustainable) infrastructure.

Specifically, we must focus on decentralization of utilities and modular construction methods that can scale quickly. Examples of these development techniques can already be seen in Asia and Africa because of the drastic need for more housing for rapidly growing populations.

Cryptocurrency

I save this section for last, not because it is the least important, but because it is the most, and I have deep personal knowledge and experience in this market, more than any other covered previously here. Crypto presents us with the greatest wealth building opportunity of our generation. This is not hyperbole. The numbers speak for themselves. While I won't go into the basics of cryptocurrencies and blockchain here, the reader is encouraged to do her own research into the subject. A few hours of internet research will make you an expert compared to the average person because, while gaining popularity, crypto is still not well understood by most people and mass media coverage has been decidedly biased and dumbed down.

Blockchain is the next evolution in the Internet Age and the ramifications of this technology haven't even been fully explored, but we do know that monetary systems, data storage/processing, supply chain, decentralized governance, education, and decentralized energy/power systems are all areas that blockchain is prepared to disrupt.

However, as an asset class, which is what we're interested in exploring here, cryptocurrencies and crypto assets provide the potential for asymmetric returns, so with relatively little investment capital, one can generate large absolute returns. It would take quite a while to create generational wealth in the stock market with just $1,000 starting capital without using leverage. In the crypto world, $1,000 can create a substantial nest egg in relatively short order. For example, when I bought my first bitcoin in 2013, a $1,000 investment starting on September 1, 2013, would now be worth $52,433 on September 1, 2018. And that's not even that impressive.

During the last major bull run, I bought a coin right before a massive pump and dump called Dentacoin (DCN), and over the period of one week made 84 times my initial investment. So a $1,000 investment would have been worth $84,000 in one week, with no leverage. The crypto market is fraught with these opportunities, although it is becoming increasingly crowded and difficult to differentiate various projects, and the market is also rife with scams.

Nevertheless, with diligent research, sound strategies, and cooperatively pooling our resources, the Black community can come together and create generational wealth for those of us with the vision to capitalize on these opportunities before mainstream adoption. At minimum every Black person and organization should have a diversified portfolio comprised of the top cryptocurrencies and just hold them as a long-term investment while rebalancing the portfolio regularly.

There are many small crypto groups that have popped up to serve the Black community. Most are simple group chats that share information or investment pools that opportunistically seek deals on a piecemeal basis. As mentioned before, BlacKrypto

Society is the first group with a well-developed strategic plan and cryptocurrency to help the Black community collectively invest in and build crypto/blockchain projects, prioritizing, but not limited to, Black-owned blockchain initiatives, and an overall roadmap that ties various projects together that may not even seem connected if you don't understand the bigger picture. From the BlacKrypto Society blackpaper, "Rather than being a blockchain company focused on a particular niche, we are building a collective where Black people around the world can use blockchain to practice ujamaa (cooperative economics), build wealth, and promote/advance Afrikan culture." Whether through BlacKrypto Society or other collectives, crypto should hold a place in any investment portfolio.

CONCLUSION

This work is intended to be a high level strategic overview and I tried to make it as short as possible. Specific development plans would need to be put in place on a country-by-country and organization-by-organization basis. The plan is to write a follow up to this book with case studies from at least three organizations and three countries. This is a call out to any organizations or countries that would like to participate, even if they do not want to be included in the next book. To participate, please reach out through intheblack2050.com.

The Black community cannot continue to ignore basic economic realities and expect to make any progress. The time to act has long past.

In the immortal words of Marcus Mosiah Garvey:

Up, up, you mighty race. You can accomplish what you will!

ABOUT THE AUTHOR

Tre Baker started his first company at the age of 19 and has built a diverse array of entrepreneurial and corporate experience throughout his professional career. His corporate experience includes various roles at Brown-Forman, and renewable energy commercialization at General Electric. As an entrepreneur, he has founded/operated several companies in consulting, retail/e-commerce, entertainment, and blockchain. He is currently engaged in business development consulting and investment management services targeted at startup companies and small businesses, through which he has worked in the telecom, biofuels, mobile/web apps, automotive, real estate, cryptocurrency, and commodities trading industries.

Tre holds a degree from Vanderbilt University in Engineering Science, Management of Technology, with minors in Finance and Corporate Strategy, an MBA from Harvard Business School, and is a licensed real estate agent in Georgia. He is also a member of Alpha Phi Alpha Fraternity, Inc., and the Emerging 100 of Atlanta, Inc. Tre was born and raised in Kentucky, and currently resides in Atlanta, GA.

SUGGESTED READING

Akbar, Na'im. *Breaking the Chains of Psychological Slavery.*

Akbar, Na'im. *Know Thyself.*

Anderson, Claud. *PowerNomics.*

Baruti, Mwalimu. *Eureason.*

Cress-Welsing, Frances. *The Isis Papers.*

Garvey, Marcus. *Philosophy and Opinions of Marcus Garvey*

Jenkins, Carol. *Black Titan: A.G. Gaston and the Making of a Black American Millionaire.*

Williams, Chancellor. *The Destruction of Black Civilization.*

Williams, Chancellor. *The Rebirth of African Civilization.*

Wilson, Amos. *Blueprint for Black Power.*

Printed in Great Britain
by Amazon